# PRAISE FOR *THE LIGHT KNOWS TRICKS*

'Jo Hemmant's first collection moves between the down-to-earth and the unearthly with agility, humour and sure-footedness. From her wounded earth, "a banged gong", emerges an array of voices—those who inhabit hearty, visceral bodies and those who yearn to. This is poetry as a plucky, embodied adventure into the world of conjurors, mediums, escapologists and other supernormal magicians, like mothers and lovers, and its tightly-crafted and teasing spell leaves a longing for change in its wake. The tone crackles and the language catches alight in this unafraid and startling debut.'

— **Cherry Smyth, author of** *Test, Orange* **(Pindrop Press, 2012)**

'*The Light Knows Tricks* doesn't read like a first collection at all. It's too accomplished for that; too various. In one of her poems, she imagines death as stepping "out of myself,/ a sensation not unlike/ slipping off a coat heavy with rain". These kinds of quiet, perceptive, slightly offbeat observations are what characterise this collection, which ranges across centuries, accumulates voices, and includes two dazzling sequences, one about Houdini; the other, "The First", about the conception, growth and birth of a first child. Each of them illustrates Jo Hemmant's careful talent for seeing the bizarre as intimate, and the intimate as bizarre. This is a confident, heady collection. Read it.'

— **Bill Greenwell, author of** *Ringers* **(Cinnamon Press, 2011)**

'The extraordinary reality at work in *The Light Knows Tricks*—often rendered by arresting, sometimes devastating, detail—shows a poet fully engaged with the transformative powers of poetry; here are poems that fizz and hum and reel with the variousness of life. There are personal poems of dark unsettling directness, and in the many poems that take on the wider world, including a remarkable sequence of poems spoken by the Houdinis, we hear a poet unafraid to take on different voices to explore what they have to say to her, to us. Often these poems take us towards some kind of revelation; things do not conclude, they do not console. That is not what is on offer here— instead it is the wonder of a world constantly throwing up surprises that this poet is deft and alert enough to catch and spin, have us see as real.'

— **Greta Stoddart, author of** *Salvation Jane* **(Anvil Press, 2008)**

'With great poise and ease, Jo Hemmant explores and exposes both the personal and the universal. In voices as fluid as rain, her intense and confident writing unpicks human endurance, twists of memory, loss. This is an assured debut collection, intellectually engaging, flawless, totally accessible.'

— **Abegail Morley, author of** *Snow Child* **(Pindrop Press, 2011)**

# THE LIGHT KNOWS TRICKS

Jo Hemmant

Doire Press

First published in March 2013.

Doire Press
Aille, Inverin
Co. Galway
www.doirepress.com

Cover design & layout: Lisa Frank
Cover image: *Garment* by Peter White,
Oil, acrylic, wax. 140 X 110cm
Author photo: Ellen Montelius

Printed by Clódóirí CL
Casla, Co. na Gaillimhe

ISBN 978-1-907682-21-6

# ACKNOWLEDGEMENTS

Thanks to the editors of the following publications in which some of these poems first appeared: *Iota, Magma, Dream Catcher, Brittle Star, The New Writer, Horizon Review, Obsessed with Pipework, Fire, Norwich Writers' Circle 41ˢᵗ Open Poetry Competition Anthology 2012, nothing left to burn* (Ragged Raven, 2011), *Terra Pax* (Cinnamon, 2011), *Jericho* (Cinnamon, 2012).

The sequence 'The First' won first prize in *The New Writer* Poetry and Prose Competition 2011 (collection category); 'Interview with a Chilean Miner' won second prize in the Torriano Poetry Competition, 2012; 'Kingscote's Man' won third prize in the Kent and Sussex Open Poetry Competition 2011; 'The Portreeve's House, East Street' was a runner-up in the Cardiff International Poetry Competition 2012; a selection of poems was highly commended in the Doire Press Chapbook Competition 2012; a selection of poems was highly commended in *The New Writer* Poetry and Prose Competition 2011; 'In the Pool' was highly commended in the Norwich Writers' Circle 41ˢᵗ Open Poetry Competition; 'Translation' was highly commended in *The New Writer* Poetry and Prose Competition 2011 (single poem category); 'Looking for Mother' was highly commended in the Northampton Literature Group Poetry Competition 2011; 'Disorder' was commended in the Torriano Poetry Competition 2012.

Huge thanks are owed to Bill Greenwell, Cherry Smyth, Abegail Morley and Greta Stoddart; to Myra Schneider and her poetry group; to John Walsh and Lisa Frank. And thanks too to my family, here and there.

# CONTENTS

*For Theo and Michael.*

# An Engine Room off the Coast of North Africa

The asbestos lagging on the pipes
has split and burst. As the engineer peels it back,
dust rises, floats across the room —
a woman's ghost, a chiffon negligée,
reminder of what they've missed.

The men laugh, crack jokes,
a skinny lad from Formby
pulls her in for a dance. At his touch,
she shivers, breaks into a cloud
of dandelion clocks — leaving them
an empty shroud, a story to write home,
traces of her bedded down
in the folds of their lungs.

# In the Dining Room

there are silver candlesticks,
napkin rings, a decanter of port,
diminutive cruet set. There are birds.

A barn owl comes in to land
over their heads. A moorland watercolour
is the backdrop for the hawk in his glass case.

Gulls hunch on the sideboard's edge
ready to dive-bomb the Royal Doulton.
On the windowsill a pheasant struts,

breast gold as her wedding ring,
white collar the halo she finds
when she slips it off. This one he bagged.

Words lodge in her throat,
a pellet of small bones, teeth, fur.

# Close

A man's head
through the space between seats.

Shaved, each follicle
a dark dot

like a speckled egg,
a pen and ink. Swaying

slightly, a gymnast
up-ended on a beam.

I want to reach out,
feel the nap of new hair,

stroke the ridge of scar
behind one ear. Unpick the seam.

# Power-Cut

The blue burn of the gas fire
with its whiff of dentist's chair,
a wash from a bowl on the rug, facecloth's
rough touch, water tepid, outside a fog so thick
we can't make out the neighbours.
This is adventure.

When the doorbell rings, she hesitates:
who calls during a power-cut
and a pea-souper at that?
She peers through frosted glass, whispers,
*It's a man and woman.*

Spun from fog, coming in to warm themselves
by our gas fire, the only one in the road.
They'll kneel down before its hiss and singe,
flimsy as ghosts. Hold out hands
that flicker like candle flames.
Disappear.

# Scratch Days

Now and then we have to let ourselves in,
knowing before we've unlocked the door
that inside it's as if no-one's home —

TV off, radio quiet as the hush
between each tick of the kitchen clock,
the only sound a distant rat-a-tat-tat.

She's up in the box room
with towers of tins stockpiled
against famine and flood, hunched

over the Singer, feeding swags of polycotton
across its cool, metal plate
while the frenzied needle stabs,

retreats. Pins clamped between her lips
like threats, foot down like a racing driver
accelerating out of a corner's rubber stink.

# Down Our Road

At twilight the women go out
into the brewing dark. Backs
to their houses, arms folded

against their hearts, they cool
like the cups of tea
there's never time to drink.

No-one turns to speak.
Faces blank as mannequins,
they stand as if mesmerised

by a moustached Svengali
pacing the back path
with a fob watch.

After a moment or two,
they tilt their heads, discover
the first star's out

bright as a naked bulb
and the day runs off their backs
like water, seeps into the ground.

# Pastimes

On the hob, a ham hock pink as sunburn
in a slurry of peas. On the radio,
Sinatra. She's singing along,

a perky quickstep in her heels.
Soon she'll make a pot of tea and,
one eyebrow levitating like a swami,

share a scandal from the paper
or pull out a piece of gossip
that's been gathering lint in her pocket

for weeks. Once she's off, I'll egg her on,
get her to tell me again
about the bombs that brought houses

to their knees, the Anderson shelters,
flash GIs, contraband Irish beef
Great-uncle Mick smuggled in.

Last week I learned to draw stocking lines
rope-trick straight; the lost art
of a good carrot marmalade.

# What Would Father Paul Say?

The first bides
its time in her mouth
like a secret.

The others girls salt their talk with it.
She knows the fact she doesn't
has been noted,
will be used against her.

She tries it out in the bathroom mirror,
turns on the tap, parts her lips,
eases air out into an *fffff*, squeezes
a guttural *uh* from her throat
before bending her tongue back on itself
to form the *ck* —

leaving room for another
that makes her mouth water
like a sweet sucked
to a thin pane of glass.

# Chaperone

Tipsy on a swig of Cinzano and lemonade,
you watch the local hunk

send halos of smoke
to the ceiling of his garden shed —

his left hand in your mate's lap
like a cat; like opportunity.

He passes you his soggy roll-up;
you can't reel your smile in fast enough

and, as the Sex Pistols shriek
'Frigging in the Rigging', he moves in

for the kill, the lyrics as daring
as him squeezing the 34Cs

you'd give anything to have.
She doesn't object.

The words *enough's enough*
lounge around in your throat.

# Wardrobe

Plump satin hangers
in baby pink and peppermint
are shoulders for beaded cocktail gowns,

chiffon negligées, a silk kimono
the colour of cherry stains,
cool as a draught to the touch.

Shelves of unscuffed shoes
in burgundy, black patent, bottle green
ache to be filled. She slips in

her feet, teeters on stilettos
as she reaches for the heavy fur
with its feral scent,

the candy-striped boxes of hats
with plumes, peaks, feathers,
brims. In a pillbox with a stiff veil,

she paints on a cupeybow, powders
her face, becomes a movie star
from the matinées they watch

on Saturday afternoons.
Last week Errol Flynn materialised
in a shirt unbuttoned to the waist.

Moustache tickling, he kissed her
as if she wasn't thirteen,
uncomfortable in her skin.

# Geography

My last report mentioned *worrying gaps in her knowledge.*
I try to pay attention but the sky's matted with clouds

the wind corrals, borders constantly shifting — unlike
the countries on the antique globe we're forbidden to touch.

*Cumulus.* A cash crop of cotton bolls sodden with rain
that might have been pumped from Australia's

Great Artesian Basin or evaporated from the cool green
meltwater of a glacier's paddled foot. A cargo train trundles past

towing containers labelled Kuehne and Nagel, Maersk.
I want to lie flat on its cast-iron roof, cling on till we reach

a place I've never heard of, check into a hotel
with a birdcage elevator where I'll have an illicit rendezvous

in a stolen identity before heading out to explore.
The flank of a dark cloud makes the striplight stand out.

All I'll remember of Russia is the delicious word *archipelago.*
That its schoolchildren are taught propaganda.

# The Great Houdini

## 1. Provenance

There's hush as the ringmaster introduces the opening act:
Les Aerialistes, trapeze artists all the way from Paris, France —
six women in daring satin corsets with tail feathers, who swing over

our heads on tiny seats, gathering momentum, bodies bucking
and arching like kites. I will them to let go and they do,
a collective wheeze as the first girl sails out, a catapulted missile,

nothing but hard-packed earth beneath her, hands hooking
her partner's, who has flipped upside down, is hanging
by the knees, a slipped stitch. Together they sway back and forth,

a pendulum picking up speed till the girl's released into a reel
of somersaults as spinning, as precise as the works of father's watch.
Later I'll find a clutch of nails on my palms — blue half-moons.

## 2. Give Me the Boy till He's Seven

*It was Mother taught me to be a magician. A cabbage,*
*three potatoes, the ghost of a pot roast picked clean*
*on blue and white china from Budapest.*
*A feast for her and my father, seven growing kids.*

The first time I swung
on my makeshift trapeze,
pulled off a passable back flip
from its hurtling seat —

how she said my name, *Ehhh-rich*,
as if I had taken her life away,
returned it in a new set of clothes,
face cleaned.

## 3. Magician's Assistant

I can tell you the moment we fell into place
like the perfection of a difficult trick:

I was trying my luck
on the Coney Island boardwalk

that first night, leaning in, whispering
with a con man's oily charm

how each star had been lit up just for us,
a galaxy of astrological signs. As I reached in

to kiss her cheek, something happened
I can't explain — clearer

than a memory, as choreographed
as a stunt, images of the life we'd have

hard on one another's heels
like the pages of a flick book ticking.

A wave against the sea wall brought me back,
a cold shower of salt spray. As I pulled

away, her eyes widened in shock
and I knew she'd read my mind.

## 4. Metamorphosis

You get all kinds here — at ten cents to stare
through the Human Window Pane, see a man's heart

where ordinarily he'd sport a buttonhole, its nervous twitch
too much somehow for his wasted frame;

to gawk at the bearded lady who's unnervingly polite
as she asks the men if they'd like to part the chinstrap

that's grown to her thighs, examine what's underneath;
stroke the tattooed woman's opaque skin, its circus

an opium dream in indigo; marvel as a midget lifts Bogdan
the Strong Man with ease.  But we're the reason they come:

they can't get enough of me tying Bess up, stowing her
in a trunk and with a clap of my hands

and exit stage left, she's grown five inches, changed
sex — become Houdini the showman, an imago.

## 5. Newspaper Men —

they're the trick. At Woonsocket, Rhode Island,
I invited a reporter to the stationhouse
to watch me escape a twelve-foot chain, handcuffed.
The cops were against it at first — not surprising

given I was in a leopard-skin loincloth
like a two-bit beer hall performer —
but I freed myself in under a minute,
arms pumping like pistons to hide the pin

between my pinkie and ring-finger
that I fiddled back and forth
as if prising the meat from a clam —
each lock springing in turn

with a satisfying click, the cuffs coming off
as easily as Bess shimmying out of sleeves,
falling to the floor like dollar signs;
the first words of a headline.

## 6. Illusion # 23: Indian Needle Mystery

Taught me by a Hindoo conjurer from East India
at the Chicago World Fair. Of course you don't actually
swallow, despite theatrical gnashing of teeth,

bobbing of your Adam's apple. No, you line up
the needles in a pocket inside your cheek, holes in a row,
thread the cotton through with your tongue

like knotting cherry stems while worrying the stump
of a broken tooth. Months to perfect.
But the audience go wild and, to tell you the truth,

I deserve the applause whether I swallow them or not.
Show me the tailor who can thread needles in the dark,
the blind man who reads Braille with his tongue.

## 7. More than One Way to Skin a Cat

Some afternoons I call and call his name
till it careens around the house, a dove freed
from a conjurer's hat. When no answer comes, I know
I'll find him submerged in the enormous bath

he's had built, hair a dark corona, cheeks tanked
with air, those pale eyes of his pretty as sea glass.
We always play it the same. I reach past
the sucked-in stomach, the hip-bones that fit

like bookends outside my own, to his schmekel,
small and soft, floating like a Dime Museum display —
feel it stiffen, crane its neck. He surfaces then, mind on more
than stacking seconds, thumbing his nose at death.

## 8. On the Occasion of Mayer Samuel Houdini's 17th Birthday

He would be the one to invent a son.
Perhaps his greatest sleight of hand: letters
in that dramatic copperplate, *Dear Mrs Houdini,*
*Mayer has his first tooth, is crawling, can say his name,*
*in full, our boy,* tender anecdotes of bumps and scrapes —
trying to fly before he could walk, of course —
of night-time vigils, lisped funnies, tantrums, slapstick.
                            As if I'd have as little say
in my own son as I do in his act: ever the flunky;
the suspension of disbelief; the accessory after the fact.
He did allow him a likeness though — my dark eyes.
Little touches like that, they're why he's the success he is.
A locket with a wispy golden curl for Mother's Day.
A scuffed pair of calf-skin baby shoes. And when the child
would have started school, the reports began, always
in a different hand — outlining academic glory,
popularity, sporting prowess. I've even an invitation
to his bar mitzvah somewhere.
                            He has never mentioned him
to my face; realises that would be too much to stomach.
No, I find the letters on my pillow every month,
about that time; a thoughtless gift.

Note: The Houdinis often addressed each other as Mr and Mrs Houdini.

## 9. The Star

never drops his act,
lets the lights go down.

Every word is a drumroll,
every gesture a cymbal crash.

Even an empty room
is a venue of sorts, can be warmed up

in the unrelenting bid for applause.
And the most ordinary activities —

reading quietly,
*An educated man,*

climbing the stairs,
*Look at the shape he's in,*

buttering toast,
*Such dextrous hands,*

are carried out as if
the audience of the Hippodrome are here,

spellbound.
Waiting for me to slip up.

## 10. The Upside Down

or Chinese Water Torture Cell. A mahogany and steel box,
the sides tempered, half-inch glass — designed so the roof,

fitted with stocks, can be hoisted off, my ankles bolted in
before they crank me up to the ceiling feet first, a side of beef

on a butcher's hook, lower me into the tank like bait. The curtains
are swished across — this, every medium knows, adds to the suspense —

and there I hang in the amniotic dark, on the run from every shop,
building site, stockyard and steelworks in the US of A.

Meditation's the key. My mantra unpicks any lock, a beelike hum
as I reach up and begin my most sensational escape:

*Ehrich meet Harry; Harry, Ehrich: the little Jewish kid from Budapest
who's made it bigger than the Flatiron Building.*

In precisely two minutes I'll stagger onto the stage,
wet and breathless as a newborn, bring them to their feet.

## 11. Looking for Mother

As in my line of work, it's all in the details:
the lights as low as a poor man's bordello;
a Tarot pack fanned out on a damask cloth;
the aromatic burn of incense to focus the mind

on higher things, a round of cognacs. When she seats us,
I insist we're as tightly packed as immigrants in steerage
so any chicanery will be telegraphed around the table.
*Are you there, Walter?* she asks, voice tremulous,

*Are you there?* And there's nothing I want more
than to see some fellow from the beyond
materialise in a skein of ectoplasm, float about the room
with the luminous grace of a jellyfish.

But I haven't met a medium yet I couldn't debunk.
We hear a whisper, a man's jaunty whistle
as if he's just come in after a hard day's work.
Overwhelmed, she insists on a break

and here's the schtik: lights up, lights quickly down
then a bell rings, a mirror cracks and a china dog
hits my neighbour on the head.
Mrs Cranden, of course, is in a trance.

## 12. A Magician Among the Spirits

My one perfected act: to blow
the capricious flame of the candle
that keeps vigil beside my portrait — it darts
and gutters before springing back
as I used to.

Here every man jack is a magician, a trickster.
They know they were my patsies, schmucks
held back by the gravity of their imaginations,
and taunt me, walking a tightrope
across the brass fender of our bed.

The weight of the earth is killing, Bess.
And as with that terrible trick, I lost my north,
trapped six feet down until my heart's lode
led me up to light, to you.

These women you visit with their cabinets
and rapping sticks; their incense fug —
I've put my mouth to their ears,
shouted 'Rosabelle believe' as we'd arranged,
but they're deaf.

I'd pushed against this caul for years,
as unable to penetrate it as those mystics are
to scry a crystal ball, till just now, watching
you pin your hair, I felt such tenderness
it ghosted my veins, gave me greater resolve —
like the final few moments of the Milk-Can Escape,
lungs a pair of empty mailbags, the last of my air

a flurry of bubbles, my shoulders slipping their sockets
as easily as they'd shrug off a greatcoat; a question.

Our cipher leaves my mouth,
a key to your world. The flame goes out.
You turn, look straight through my illusion.
Believe, Bess, believe.

Note: *The weight of the earth is killing* is a line from Houdini's diary
referring to his 'Buried Alive' act.

# Interview with a Chilean Miner

What kept me sane? Astral travel.
You look skeptical but I'm not the only one
to have talked of how it is down there:

go far enough, you actually feel the earth throb —
she's like a wound; a banged gong. At night
I'd lie on the floor, nothing between

me and her, a tablet on a tongue, meditate
until every bone and muscle dissolved
and I could float on a raft of magnetic waves

through 2,000 feet of rock into the night,
the air clean and cold as spring water. I'd only
to point my arms towards Copiapo's lights

and out I'd fly; over the desert scrub into town,
over luckier men stumbling home
till I was the wrong side of our door

which I'd rush like blood through a valve —
greeted by the smell of rice and beans still warm
on the stove, the radio on for company.

She'd be asleep in our room, a series of bumps
under the quilt. I'd slip in, spoon to her egg, giddy
at the peppery nape of her neck, the nest of damp curls.

I'd fight sleep but it always won. That
was the worst of it: to wake up next to Gomez,
his arm across my chest, strapping me in.

# Picking Him Up

The camellia's in bloom, a Whitsun parade
of froth and flounce. I walk down the drive,
over the kerb's split lip, the hole in the road
made by the weight of snow, the insinuation
of ice, past the half-built house. Up ahead
a woman is pushing a pram, skirt flighty as washing
on a line. Her baby's blue shoe balances on the tip
of his toes as his arms direct the cars that shush by.
Their movement carries me on, past post office,
chiropodist, redbrick and sandstone villas
to the traffic lights where the helicopter landed
the day the postman lost his leg, blades still ticking
as the crowd filmed with their mobile phones.
To the Halfway: hairdresser's, nail parlour, off-licence
barred like the Wild West, bric-a-brac.
And there's the shop front. Unmarked granite
headstone on AstroTurf, etched on the glass:
*Open 24 hours. Personal service.*
                    I'll have to ask for him by name,
as if he might get up from where I saw him last,
take my arm, walk me home.

# Inviting Him Back from the Dead

On the afternoon in question,
I make sure everyone's out, slip on

a new dress, put Nat and his velvet croon
in charge of ambience.

At three o'clock prompt, the bell.
Dad stands there smiling, relaxed, breathing

on his own. No rasp, no god-awful
lung-pinking cough. Says *Cheer up,*

*Sweet, it might never happen.*
It already has.

So much to talk about and I act
as if I only saw him last week, bang on about

the price of petrol, where Liverpool are
in the Premier League.

He sits quietly, smiling, not saying much.
I understand. He needs to adjust —

to gravity, a body's weight,
the clock's steady pulse.

# Spice

In a sharply pressed kurta
white as the glare from the sun,
he opens the door of his van

onto fifty, sixty sacks of onions
stacked like shelves of books, bulbs
shrugging off their brown paper skins

in readiness for the pot.
Stiff knees bent, he hoists a sack
into a hump, and the onions jounce

into the Brandon Tandoori,
its flaking gold-leaf name a promise
of floral carpets, plush velvet chairs,

nap worn to a shine, a plastic
palm tree's shade. After lunch
he'll peel and slice

enough for every dish, his face
a dry riverbed in rain.
At his side, his wife will slit

the bellies of chillies, remove their guts,
crush cumin, coriander seeds,
cardamon pods to a fiery dust,

sear chicken and lamb —
spread out their dastarkhwan
on the salty Norfolk breeze.

Note: A dastarkhwan is Persian for a feast or dining cloth.

# Den

For his sixth birthday, a tent.
Two-man, pop-up. He puts it up
in his room, begs me to read to him there
that night. Crawling in, I notice how
the millimetre-thin skin cuts out noise, the air's
new with polymers. We shine a moon on the roof
with the torch, find ourselves in a field,
staring up through a plastic square at a sky
deep and dark as a coal mine's throat.

Outside the fire has cooled to amber.
Menace trip-traps through the woods.

# The Dangers of Thinking Out Loud

We're revising the past tense in French
when I explain to my son

that the present doesn't really exist.
He frowns, perturbed. I don't back up.

I tell him to envisage the past as the word
he's just said, thought he's just had

and the future as the word or thought
that comes next. 'Language is a matrix of sorts —

like air.' He perks up now, asks,
'As in the film? Can I watch it?'

And my no is an echo and a prophecy.
I reach over, pull him to me, his hard, thin body

all awkward joints, long bones —
interstices.

He is the present, a between boy,
his body the space between words.

I can feel his heart beating, faster than mine,
hurrying him on — though he'll not catch me,

he's of a different time. His pulse
is the present ticking on.

# Revisiting

A village of terraced houses
that loosened its belt,
became a housing estate.

But take the ginnel
at the bottom of Moss House Lane
and you end up

in open countryside; field upon field
like a rolled-out bolt of cloth
before the iron

of the haberdasher's hand.
Turn right at the canal,
follow it to the pithead,

the wheel that worked the cage
a stopped clock. Without a wind,
you can still hear

the scrawp and clink of miners
at their seams, their wives
skirls of dust, currents of air

in cottages knocked through, done up.
At tea-time they drift through windows,
under doors, gather at the head

of the lane, a low-lying mist —
wait for their men to trudge home
in the last fault of light.

# Five Days Before Christmas

*i.m. Mickey*

She falls, sweeping up leaves,
six inches from the step, shatters
her hip. No-one hears her call.

By dusk, she's haggling with God,
drifting in and out
of consciousness till she gives up,

flies onto the neighbour's roof
to stare out over the park
where she walked the dogs,

the graffitied town centre,
the moors, mines, converted mills;
becomes bolder, soars up towards

the clean plate of the moon.
She tells me this in hospital
while I comb the lugs from her hair,

dab at her dirty face with a wad
of cotton wool — trying to make me forget
the night outside; remember her

doing aerial somersaults,
flipping like a Russian gymnast
from star to star.

# Limbo

They have to cut through
the corset of cat gut

to open me up again and I find
I can simply step out of myself,

a sensation not unlike
slipping off a coat heavy with rain,

letting it fall to the floor.
Helium-light, I drift to the ceiling

and float, a nebula, fascinated
as a young doctor reaches in,

takes hold of my heart
like a handful of water he mustn't spill,

squeezes the blood through himself.
It refuses to beat.

A woman notes the time.
They stand back, an army in retreat.

Where's the promised tunnel?
The white light?

The tea lady's on her way.
I can hear the cups rattle, her cheery,

*Hello my love, what's it to be?*

# An Englishman's Castle is His Home

He's rooted to the kerb,
the man in the anorak and woolly scarf,
his torn trousers held up by string, hipbone
a stropped blade. It's June, thirty degrees.
I try not to breathe, worry he'll notice
but his eyes are somewhere else,
unblinking, catatonic.
He's holding two things: a plastic bag in holes
and a glossy coffee table book,
edges of the jacket frayed,
title: *At Home at Castle Howard.*

That's where he is — strolling across
a striped lawn to the fizz of bees,
the sky blue as the cover. In a moment
he'll turn right at the walled garden,
find a summer house, take tea in the shade.

Later, after a light supper in the library,
he might decide on the Grey Room
and in paisley silk pyjamas
slip into a four-poster bed, sheets
newly pressed, sprinkled with lavender water.
Sleep the sleep of the damned.

# The Donation

As soon as the anaesthetic wore off,
I knew something was wrong. As if my head
had been split into two — a house turned into flats,
someone upstairs who at first was nothing more
than a slammed door, the scrape of a chair
then I'd find a bike propped in the hall, a parcel on a console
peppered with foreign stamps.

                How my body feels now?
The best analogy is a borrowed coat on a night out,
shoulders boxy, arms too long. I used to move
with a dancer's grace: fluid; elegant. Now I walk
with a cocksure strut, chew gum, sit with my knees
far apart as bookends. I've begun to mumble when I talk
and my hands no longer accentuate my words.
Last week I packed up the classical box-sets,
put them on eBay while Charles was at work,
downloaded hard rock onto a brand-new iPod.

                Did I mention the nightmares?
The rush of racing a Suzuki down a dual carriageway
when a juggernaut in the next lane starts to drift
sideways, careers into the central reservation? I swerve,
the bike catches the tailgate and I'm doing a pirouette,
an uprooted tree in the eye of a tornado. I wake
drenched in sweat, the thud of my new heart
loud as the smack of a head on tarmac.

                I'm off to Brighton this weekend.
To a pastel blue mid-terrace house I've never seen.
To the corner of Wycliffe and Albion, where I'll find
a gang of lads smoking, knocking back warm cider
from a passed-round can. Not quite ready to stand
closer together, close the gap; mention his name.

# Familiars

You see them everywhere,
couples who could easily
be related by blood.
Each a blurry half
of a Rorschach blot,
Narcissus rooted
to the bank of a pool —
love in the fervent cling
of polar molecules.

As if they searched
until they caught a glimpse
across a platform, a pulsing
dance floor, of their own faces,
slightly skewed. Their subconscious
a seductive whisper
in a ready ear:
they can trust themselves,
can't they?

# Spellbound

You follow the skirts of hedgerows
out to the salt flats. Mud, marsh grass, the sift

of silt, here you are part of the earth, its craft:
where a hare runs a white-tailed round,

mark it out. Gather skullcap, rosemary and orris root
to trick a foolish heart. Move to him through shadow —

crow, cat, witch, the scent of silk, its slink
and skin's quick warmth. In the morning

he will wake tongued, tied, a pentacle,
your ropes the guise of love.

# The Guest

At night she holds a vigil next to my bed.
Mouth and nose quiet

under a cupped hand,
I can hear her wheeze, smell

her cocoa butter scent.
Summoned, Mother says *You*

*and your imagination*
but as she goes back downstairs,

the room turns winter cold
and a frost intricate as lace

blooms on the mirror like breath.
She sours new milk, leaves

scalloped fingerprints on fruit,
tars food to the bottom of pans.

An apocryphal tale,
statue that weeps blood,

magician's sleight of hand, I wake
to the crack and spit of flames,

undertow of smoke
but with the lamp on, can't see a thing.

# The Portreeve's House, East Street

The ghosts of port wardens are assessing, repossessing
our creaking Tudor home.  In Flemish cloth

and Mandarin silks that sailed into port on caravels,
they stalk the worn oak boards, pausing to count

the knots in Persian rugs, finger fabrics,
note the range and clarity of colours, the skill.

In the pantry they take inventories, admire the utility of tins,
scrutinise labels, modern ingredients conundrums

they cannot solve. Spices run through their fists like time,
perfuming every room. They catalogue wines, marvel

at the New World, calculate taxes, voices clear as a radio.
We find tea leaves in mounds on the kitchen scales,

hand-written levies tucked in the tops like flags.
When visitors call, practised hands slide into pockets,

palm unfamiliar coins, dismiss notes, exact their due.
What's locked or closed must be divulged — drawers

turned out, letters read, conversations attended to.
We pretend that the scratch of nibs in ledgers is mice,

their interest in us an infestation in the timbers;
ignore movements at the corners of our eyes.

# Translation

Up a hill as steep as a back in a loveless bed
we pull into Orage, a word we remember
from schoolbook French. A dozen houses
in stone the colour of wet sand, geranium
window boxes, shutters bleached by the sun,
absolute quiet that makes you remark
you could not live in rural France

while I'm imagining a scene: at night
the women come out, tongues soused in vinegar,
barbed on a husband's edge, serve up grudges
with a clatter of cast-iron pots. In the orchard,
barrel-chested men fight bare-knuckle, fists
accurate as compass needles, and their roars
knock the stars from the gods — *storm*.

# Lincoln's Inn Fields

November trees do their best to hide
the night's orange cast. Note the Baroque railings

that border the square, the fog that dulls
the amber of the faux gas lamps, the Gothic redbrick

turrets and towers of the law — a pair
of barristers, wigged and frocked, a nice touch.

You could be in Victoria's London, silk hems buoyed
over cobblestones, the clacking one-two of heels

hooves conjuring the hollow roll of wooden wheels
as a hansom brisks past. Air is antique with wood-smoke,

the froth and spill of ale, slap and spit of chops.
From dogleg alleys, a volley of whistles and calls.

The doors are locked on Hunter's ghouls.

# Kingscote's Man

I used to sleep on a bench, wake stiff and cold
as hung meat. Now my truckle's wheeled out last thing,
put at the foot of his bed, an ornate shoe's
scuffed tip. The chaff pricks more holes in my back

than the fleas suck. There's a fustian blanket
rough as a mother scouring skin, a wheedling draft.
Master sleeps behind a baudekin spun from
gold and silks, the colour of a candle flame.

The coverlet tucked under his quiver of chins
is trimmed with fur. Beneath his noble arse
a featherbed I beat twice a day
with a flagellant's care, two canvas bags

stuffed with flock in a four-post frame.
Once, belly afire from an excess of suckling pig,
he bade me climb up to put it out,
my hand rubbing his gut

like a maid looking for the shine in brass.
When he dozed off, I lay down, floated into sleep
on God's own cloud, cosseted as an infant
in the crook of an arm. I dreamed of home,

six of us sleeping cheek to flank
like the sweet swivel of socket and bone,
our warmth, our sour smell, his frequent
roils and belches dragging me back.

# Notes on a House

You fix her, from leaking roof to rotted sill.
Woo her with passed-down furniture, threadbare rugs.
Spend money you don't have on period paints: *clunch,*
*savage ground, mouse's back, lamp room grey.*

Scour junkyards for brass door knobs, ornate lights
with teardrop bowls. Rip plywood off to uncover
fireplaces, hand-painted tiles, the bones of birds
ominous. In the brambles there's a claw-footed

cast-iron bath pitted as a peach stone. It is yours
for the mending. Slowly the house comes back to life.
Bars of music, tail-ends of conversations flit like moths
across high-ceilinged rooms. Bells ring out, velvet pulls

swinging like the hanged. Grates are swept, fires set, mahogany
beeswaxed. Vases you don't own appear, choked with phlox.
You step over the chilly sixth stair as if it's a pavement crack.
Your face in the crackle glaze mirror startles itself.

# To Make Certain What You Loved of Me is Yours

You will find me in dark water
where bridge shadows dance,

blue-wet,
swollen with expectation —

belly, breasts.
Bring the oyster knife,

my eyes are amethysts.
Bring scissors to shear my hair for rope,

a needle and thread
and there where you lay a thousand times,

stitch me closed
then let me slide again into water —

the kiss of fish to undress me,
loose my bones.

# Sailor's Blood

Two years is my limit. Then I notice how loud
the latch is when it clicks into place,
how furniture has slipped its moorings

to drift to the centre of rooms.
Just decorated walls inch forward, rafters
tighten their grip, force floating ceilings

to sink, the floor a swell rising
to meet them. The view that sold it
stifles; the drive's no longer a way in

but an exit strategy. You baulk, complain
about stamp duty, list the benefits
of putting down roots. It's no use —

you're with a woman whose mind's eye
is a telescope lens, a porthole, plotted
like a compass face. I wake from dreams

of steering into a port clogged with skiffs,
air humid with a language I don't speak —
have to lift the blind, stare out

into a dark I can never fathom.

# How to Reclaim Your Former Self

Feel free to undress —
the light knows tricks.

Walk about the room, pique his interest
before you lift the sheet,

slide in. Remember, the sea is in you,
you are nothing but water, tidal,

as his fingers swirl and eddy
across the salty membrane of your skin.

Each kiss will make fish gather
in ticklish shoals, electric eels arc

and flare, whales sing to you
in a bewildering baritone.

Lie still, let seaweed wrap slippery fronds
around your wrists, tether you

as he slips in and out, his mouth
holding your name like air.

You are current. Squall.
Undertow.

# Travelling Backwards

It's a classic — cherry red, lights
Cuban cigars, tail fins, white vinyl roof.

I picture myself in the front, gloved hands
smoothing the satin bell of a dirndl skirt,

knees whisper-close, wind whistling through
a handle-turn of the window,

back-combed hair lacquered still. Smitten,
I decide to try on this retro girl

and shoulders back, chin up, sweet smile
painted on, we stroll up the high street, steps

short on account of the kitten heels that tick
like a mantel clock. We are light as sun.

We buy flowers, cold cream, a blue silk scarf
that catches our eye like a scrap of sky, knots

jauntily at the throat, take tea and cake in a café
where distracted by the next table,

I lose my grip and she drifts up
with the steam from our china cup —

ankles crossed, pinky at half-mast.

# Mind Over Matter

*'Inside every thin woman is a fat woman desperate to get out,'*
— Angela Carter

My therapist's solution: murder.
Week one, we worked up to a blow

to the head with a blunt instrument.
Week two, a session with a jointing knife

and into the water she went — seasoned
with bay leaf, a handful of juniper berries,

salt and pepper. Week three we watched
the flesh slip from her bones

slow and sure as a striptease.
The highlight of week four: the fat frothing

on top of the pot like cream;
an hour more to skim it with a ladle.

At our final meeting, we dished her up
onto best china, charged our glasses

with a good red, drank to restraint.
Of course, she's still with me — whenever I pass

Bachmann's Patisserie; in the puff of a sleeve,
unexpected billow of a skirt.

# Disorder

Mrs Maynard is finished. Every ornament's been lifted,
swabbed with the lambswool duster, put back exactly
where it was, every wooden surface daubed with beeswax,
rubbed till her face is a ghost of itself
and the word luster, all kettle-whistling 'ssss',
springs to mind. She has vacuumed under furniture,
over rugs — tassels coaxed into a military line —
bent dimpled knees, girded loins to lift the sofa,
plate-glass coffee table which she purged of fingerprints
as though it were the scene of a crime. The final task:
to plump the Waterford silk cushions she treated herself to
that summer, the kapok a disappointment given the price
but they do hold their shape. Half-past.
She eyes the dining room like it's the last man on earth,
strikes a bargain with herself: a cup of tea, a crunch cream
after she's blacked the grate, wiped the skirting boards twice.
Then she'll venture upstairs. Does she deserve a bath?
She tries to dislodge an image of a tidemark and rats' tails of hair
with breasts floating pink and pretty as water lilies. Perhaps.

# The First

## 1. The Umpteenth Cycle

Flat on my back,
legs splayed in the air
in an athletic V,
hands under my arse
angling my hips, I subject
your slippery deposit
to gravity.

The frontrunner's
half swimming, half falling
down my inhospitable canal,
through the narrow window
in my cervix
into the spongy tissue
of my womb.

There he's on his own —
must thread himself
through the eye
of my kinked left tube,
find the ripe egg
which won't flinch
as he noses exhausted
through its coddled shell.

You're on the far side of the bed,
mute, still — a spent cartridge;
a smoking gun.

## 2. The Doctor Says Relax

so we take a holiday in France
where you make me an accidental gift:
the lifecycle of the cicada —

how the female scrapes slits in bark,
lays clutches of eggs like caviar
from which nymphs hatch,
burrow deep
                underground —
a doped colony
suckling on tree roots
for up to seventeen years.

In the final instar
they bubble up like ground oil,
moult, emerge singing,
ready to mate.

### 3. Symptomatic

The first thing I notice
is the sharpness of must
but can find no trace of mould
on the pristine magnolia walls.

The patch will appear later —
for now the hyphae are dividing,
multiplying in moist cavities
in the brick and plaster;
a growing network of filaments
this side of a broken gutter,
dispersing spores like a lung.

Later the tidemark will creep,
the wallpaper paunch
with the weight of water.

## 4. Steerage

(i)

my breasts and belly
are fuller, rounder —
sails in a tailwind
                    carrying me out
over the water.

A poor sailor, I heave up
my diet of ship's biscuits,
ginger tea.

Soon my bones will soften,
ligaments loosen —
like halyards at full tilt.

(ii)

Hungry, thirsty,
I become disoriented —
nothing in the sextant's sights
but the skerry I passed yesterday.

I am sailing in circles,
creating a vortex.

No, a cocoon.

## 5. Hive

like field bees
transferring nectar to drones —
mouth to mouth, to build
a complex honeycomb.

I sit in state on the sofa
attuned to the hum,
the teeming of cells.

## 6. She Dreams of the Quickening

The stolen baby's asleep.
I peel off his rompa, sodden nappy,
slather him in baby oil,
lift him by the ankles,
swallow him whole —
his head crowning again
and again as he pushes through
the rings of cartilage in my throat,
settles in my stomach
like greed.

He's glad to be on the inside again:
easy food; the rush of my blood
smoothing the edges from sounds.

Soon I'll feel a jab under my ribs:
a travelling foot; the floret
of a determined fist.

## 7. The West London Chapter

of the National Childbirth Trust
meets once a week: twelve DINKs
crammed into a front room in Chiswick.
The men compensate for having to sit
on cushions at our feet
by teaching the instructor a thing or two.

The women have the agitated look of cows
that need to be milked. We circle our bumps
with fat-fingered hands: clocking —

an ancient ritual of uncertain roots;

spiders silking a web.

## 8. In the Pool

When the contractions come
there's only my belly's hard moon
waxing, waning.

I meditate my way
out of the roundness,
leave it as a buoy
to mark the spot.

I'll be a pond skater instead —
walk on water,
exploit the surface tension,
make lazy eights
over the lukewarm pool.

Toe loops are effortless now
as are the scissors of the Mazurka.
Months of heaviness, stiff joints
gone. Bliss.

I stumble on the Lutz,
regain my balance
for a polished triple axel.

You tell the midwife
I'm not myself.

## 9. Mutation

I split open
so you can emerge — unfold
into the details of the room.

      *

Sticky with vernix
they place you on my chest —
identical to the grainy
black and white photographs
of me just born.

      *

Your eyes track me constantly.
You cry
if I put you down
and when you must sleep,
it's with a hank of my hair
in your hand.

The cord is invisible;
intact.

      *

I have lost
all sense of self.

## 10. Instincts

Just born and your tiny mouth
roots at my breast.

There are things I know
without being taught:

that I must cradle
your head and neck
in the palm of my hand
when I lift you;

that I must kiss you —
to learn your scent,
make antibodies to whatever
I taste on your skin,
release them into my milk;

trace circles
on the back of your hand
to stimulate
your immune system.

Then there's the first night home —
I drift off with you between us,
wake to see your father's arm
                              falling,
a felled tree, you in its way —
put out my own arm to deflect it.

The bruise refuses to fade.

**Jo Hemmant** was born in Manchester in 1967, and this was to be the first of many places she has lived, including Sicily, Holland and Hong Kong. She has always worked with words—after brief stints teaching English as a foreign language and writing PR puffs, she moved into journalism and editing. This experience in publishing prompted her to set up Pindrop, a boutique poetry press, in 2010, which has published twelve titles to date. She now lives in the Kent countryside with her husband and two sons and is involved in local poetry, acting as Secretary of The Kent and Sussex Poetry Society and running creative writing workshops. Her poems have been published in various magazines and anthologies, such as *Magma*, *Iota, Dream Catcher, Jericho* (Cinnamon Press, 2012) and *nothing left to burn* (Ragged Raven Press, 2011) and she has won prizes in several competitions, including first prize in *The New Writer* Poetry and Prose Competition 2011(collection category), second prize in the Torriano Poetry Competition in 2011 and runner-up in the Cardiff International Poetry Competition 2012.